colcha

colcha

aaron a. abeyta

university press of colorado

Copyright © 2001 by the University Press of Colorado

Published by the University Press of Colorado
5589 Arapahoe Avenue, Suite 206C
Boulder, Colorado 80303

The University Press of Colorado is a cooperative publishing enterprise supported, in part, by Adams State College, Colorado State University, Fort Lewis College, Mesa State College, Metropolitan State College of Denver, University of Colorado, University of Northern Colorado, University of Southern Colorado, and Western State College of Colorado.

The paper used in this publication meets the minimum requirements of the American National Standard for Information Sciences—Permanence of Paper for Printed Library Materials. ANSI Z39.48-1992

Library of Congress Cataloging-in-Publication Data

Abeyta, Aaron A., 1971–
  Colcha / by Aaron A. Abeyta.
    p. cm.
  ISBN 0-87081-615-2 (pbk. : alk paper)
  1. Hispanic Americans—Poetry. I. Title.
PS3551.B48 C65 2001
811'.6—dc21

                                                                      00-012668

Designed and typeset by Laura Furney
Cover art by Marvin Muñiz

10 09 08 07 06 05 04 03 02 01   10 9 8 7 6 5 4 3 2 1

for Michele, my brilliant and beautiful wife

contents

contents

acknowledgments

i would like to thank my father, Alfonzo, for his courage, work ethic and love. my mother, Martha, for her strength, love, humor and for her understanding. both have taught me many things, and it is my hope that these poems will reflect their wisdom. also, i would like to thank my brothers and sister, Al, Anycia, and Andrew as well as the members of their loving families: Lisa, Chelsea, A.J., Adam, Jasmine, Brittany: Hal & Justin: Loriann, Rianna, Clorinda, Andrew Jr., Amber, and Amos for all of their support.

i must also thank all of my abuelitas, and abuelitos for their gift of storytelling, their love, discipline, and sense of history. these poems echo what is and was important to them, family, culture, community and much more. also, thanks to all the tios, tias, primos y primas.

a very special thanks to Bill (Guillermo) Tremblay, my friend, mentor, and wonderful writer, muchos gracias.

to all my friends, past and present, for their support. thanks to Karen, Deanna, Mark, John, Steve and all the poets and writers who helped me shape these poems.

also, a very special thanks to Mike, Alice, Miguel, Andrea, and Ana Maria, my creative and talented in-laws. thank you Michele for your inspiration and support. i love you dearly, and i could not have done this without you.

introduction: tierra

we sit in the cab of an aging 3/4 ton ford pick-up. the road in
front of us is what any country road should be, filled with ruts, wash-
boards and dust. we make our way east toward the sangre de cristos.
it is winter. my brother drives, me in the middle, and on the passenger
side sits my abuelito; his name is Amos Serafin Abeyta. at this point in
my life i am still afraid of him. he has eyes that see through people.
abuelito knows only work. six a.m. and it is time to feed the animals.
this is how i remember my childhood in moments of what needs to be
done at a certain time. the bible says that for everything there is a
time. today is our time to load the aging ford with bales of hay, alfalfa
and tasole. to the west above the san juans there are clouds gathering,
white above the peaks of white. it is the white on white of snow
gathering up its breath before it descends into the valley and blows
over the brown vegas, the newborn calves, the frozen conejos. it is
winter in canon. we, my brother and i, load the truck, seven high, 63
bales, and then we tie it with a come-a-long and a lariat that has lost its
loop. Andrew is the expert. he has always been the one my abuelito
admires. he throws the bales perfectly. one motion. they always land
where they should, how they should.
  i am the listener. i do not know enough. i struggle with the bales,
up to the thigh, turn the wrists, regroup my weight underneath myself
and heave. for a moment the bale does what it should. it is a half turn
side over side the orange twine parallel to the earth, but i have put too
much of my right arm into the lunge, the push, the heave of the 80-
pound bale. it twists in a way it shouldn't, does not sail high enough,
seven high. Andrew, left handed, reaches down and with one hand he
grabs it, places it where it should go. i am the listener. abuelito tells
me how it should have been done. how it was done in the 1930s, 40s,
50s, 60s, 70s, and how it should still be done in the 1980s. Andrew is
the worker. the left handed worker is like the mountains which surround
us, he is what my abuelito likes to look at. i am now 25 years old and
this is finally o.k. with me.
  Juan Sanchez is and was his name. he is my great grandfather,
bisabuelo. i never knew him. mogote flowered beneath his touch; with
the urging of his shovel he was able to make anything grow from this

1

rich rocky soil. bisabuelo Juan knew how to irrigate. the hay we have just finished loading is a testament to his irrigating. the fields he plowed alone, irrigated and harvested alone have made it through the decades, and they still grow. i listen. abuelito tells the story as we return with our load of hay. El Juan como puedia regar. by the time we reach canon with our teetering load we too agree that, yes, Juan Sanchez sure could irrigate. it is an art. irrigating is the brushstroke for what becomes the winter painting of two young men loading hay as their abuelito watches.

tierra means earth. everything good comes from the earth or to the earth. what travels through the air, snow, rain, sparrows, must eventually come to this field of dormant clover where 63 bales lie broken, scattered, surrounded by cows, sheep, and the ever present horses. i listen. abuelito tells us about the beauty of feeding in the same fields where the hay was harvested. the bales are full of seed and our feeding them to these pregnant cows replants the tierra. in time this earth will give birth to a windy spring and the cows will have moved south to the llano with its white sage. the earth is a protective mother. Juan Sanchez knew this.

poetry means listening. a word well thrown side over side twine parallel to the earth is a beautiful thing. 63 words well stacked, tied down and later scattered over the earth are a poem. the poem is a protective mother. Juan Sanchez can live there with the windy colorado spring, the thick rivers, the ditches, the rocky fertile soil. Amos Serafin Abeyta can become a man i no longer fear. his eyes can be something i never knew them to be. Andrew, my brother, can be proud of his work in the poem.

the snow approaches quickly from the west. it is a light snow at first. come morning there will be at least a foot. my brother and i will wake during the malignant blue of dawn. that first thin strip of blue which forms over the sangre de cristos, changes hues, then grows beyond anything the night can counter with. we will dress, go out into the cold, and both of us listen to the snow fall.

2

story

my earliest memory of trying to be a poet hovers in time like a frozen lake, my first metaphor for love. subsequent memories are often like horses. wild horses which my abuelito chased as a young man, baby doll dying that winter, thirty years old and we would not sell her to the glue man because she had been the best cow horse we had ever had. yes, the memories are a little about love and a little about death, but mostly they are those things which i cannot sell. my brother's blue hearts painted at the bottom of the sandstone cliffs which rise above my home. the home itself which was built when i was born. you see, i was born before i was a poet, and therein lies a responsibility. i have never had trouble putting down my feelings, letter upon letter, word upon word. human emotion is the second most true thing on earth; besides family it is the only thing we can always identify. emotion is our memory, that feeling when the person you love holds your hand for the first time, it is homemade jelly, elephant quilts, blue hearts, horses and the responsibility we have to recollect these things. a poem without family or emotion is, to me, nothing more than letters upon letters, the sound of hoofbeats without ever having seen a horse.

my abuelito, the oldest living person in my family, is the best poet i have ever encountered. ask me 'who is the best poet ever?' and i will not hesitate to say that his name is Amos Serafin Abeyta. i have never seen him write down one solitary word, yet his gift is language. i have never seen him read anything that is bound, yet his gift is storytelling. a poet should be a person who can tell you the same story a hundred times over and you will see it and hear it as freshly as the first time you encountered it. i have seen the wild horse that died at the end of my abuelito's rope, blue lake, where he went only once as a young man, his father, Serafin, abandoning him and his family in the 1930s. everything. i have seen everything a hundred times and have never laid eyes on any of them. the images stay with me like the scent of rain, a voice, a story, and nothing is myth.

a story is the oldest living thing on earth. as a poet, i must deal with that. there is no myth if the storyteller is good. in the time it takes to build word upon word everything becomes real. that is what i must deal with, all that is real. my name is aaron a. abeyta. i am a poet who has chosen to share all that is real to me, love, death, emotion and family. i shall put them into stories a hundred times over, one poem at a time.

antonito

here at the edge of the llano
where the grass begins
like a migrant pulse
thumping in the wind
every april
the town becomes
somebody's prayer
waiting for a candle to be lit
there are places to begin

although everything revolves
back toward us

a woman i know lost her son
and believes that he has become
a star that looks over her
i suppose this is enough

i would like to tell her
that her son
is a star
some flickering which gets confused for venus
when the nights are clear
but we both understand death too well
how we carry it
like my tio Willie
who believed he saw his dead son on t.v.

i sat listening to a friend of mine
who insisted that there was a god for everything
'yeah phone booths too   billboards   neon signs   you name it'
'third base?'
'only in the late innings when you guard the line'

that's how i think of this place
late innings
a game saving dive into the chalk

something which is never forgotten
like a bruise you wish you could show off forever

it is april here
as farmers prepare to plow
their names into the earth
and that woman still searches for her son
in the sky
the third baseman hopes he has the arm
to gun it to first

that woman i mentioned
the bruise
it's in her eyes
the wind
playing off the walls of this town
a woman waving in a mirror
bare cottonwoods swaying
and one thought flows from the other
like silent children
walking through loud kitchens

that recurring ending
a misdirected river
which always ends up
where it should
coming and going in a town
where people always return
the llano's edge
the line between us and the stars
we think we see at night

flight for life

unspoken
like morning prayers
we carry it like a medallion
around our necks

a shoestring will do
just as fine as rope
and a bullet well placed
can even sink the sun

i had a couple of primos
orale   past tense you dig

one had the horse so deep
in his veins
that he strung himself
like a wire from his cell

the other
he put a plug of lead
just above his ear

that sound had to have been louder
than the chopper
that came in the middle of the night

the old ladies were screaming
mi hijo don't die

but in the end
it was just another chopper
thick rotors
slashing the wind
like so many wrists

when the thump of echoes cleared
we named it death

for anything that lives among us
needs a name

names like Anthony   Cristobal   or chopper

we baptize every new death
with incense and a shovel
and sometimes
when the rivers get thick with spring
we follow the water downstream
and offer ourselves
to whatever god there is

a letter to Guillermo concerning why
i must write

dear Guillermo,

i feel that i must write. that there is something inside me which, like always, needs to be said, needs to be told. i look back now on the stories of my little town. the town which i cannot leave, my heart somehow held within its adobe walls. i think of the time i tripped running across the street and saw deep grooves cut into the asphalt from all those years of cruising back and forth, by all those people young and old, all of whom i know by name. it is muscles flexed for full effect, smooth necks, long hair, well sprayed being tossed like bait. these are the arms which bring me back, the beauty which keeps me.

Guillermo, it is not about the grooves in the street. it is about how they got there. they were formed by age, sun, wind and all those forces of nature we writers substitute for love and metaphor.

i think about that town, old and brown like Lara's house, which a long time ago my brothers and i tore down. how that was our last attempt at leaving, how we didn't know then what the house stood for, what the town stood for. we did not realize that when we took our hammers and shovels to it we were trying to destroy a part of our past. i thought that because we were going to plant alfalfa where it stood somehow made it all right.

i remember how we tore into that house and turned the adobe to a fine dust that clung to our skin like an old shirt. i remember that we listened to my abuelo as he told us that the field used to be more than just chamiso, how despite the rocks Lara had managed to plant grain. how now, despite the rocks, we must re-plant ourselves there.

towards the end of the day we were tired. we had taken in all the stories my abuelito offered, and with each piece of the wall crumbling the names would disappear like willow flesh from our memories. knowing that our own names would somehow be forgotten beneath the din of magpies that flew down from the cliffs to watch, to wait at the base of the mountain where long ago some lover had painted two blue hearts, now fading. as we finished, our bodies tired, we were able to walk away. i was the last to leave, a soft stepper walking on the brown skeleton of Lara's house. leaving my own name with the crumbled walls so the magpies could finally eat.

the ditches of southern colorado

perhaps the ditches
of southern colorado
do ultimately go dry
this i cannot change or revise

i think often of Cristobal
he walks the dry acequias
he is dead
does not hear the cry
that comes down from the mesa
la acequia esta viva

seven years ago
at dusk
i could hear
the distorted chords of
an electric guitar
moving through the canyon
they are what a friend of mine called
"the heart left on forever"
slow moving steps of a ghost
the work of being restless
keep walking Cristobal
this song is yours
seven years too late

el lugar de mi naciemiento

el campo santo
stares into the face of the wind
as the mounds of dirt clear their throat
and begin to erode against my skin

i have family here

on occasion
i will come up here to face the wind
to see a valley spotted with adobe birthmarks
their walls sacrificed to the cold blink of time

but the spirits
of the hands
that built them long ago
i sense that they remain
that they live in the soft skin
and fresh eyes of new generations

when i have children
i will bring them here
and point south
to show them where they began

they will help me clean abuelita's grave
to wipe the wind blown dust
from her headstone
and see the permanence of her strength
i will bring them here
para dar gracias a esperanza

cuando se secan las acequias

i remember la primavera
how the wind would appear
like a huerfano who had come home
melting the snow
and giving fresh blood to the acequia

we niños would come
flocking like grateful birds
happy to feel the cold water
run over our still smooth skin

the rancheros would come
to bless their shovels
and callused hands
in the rich mud
praying that the acequia
would last until autumn

i sat on the warm rocks
and felt the earth
moving slowly toward summer
giving up its final dust to spring

i would never grow old

now that i return
the acequia is parched
and cracked like the dry veins
of an old man's hands
maps that no one can follow
running into one another
going nowhere
the monuments of my memory
are crumbling like the old compuerta

the rancheros are gone

the niños that remain
in their eyes i see
an anemic distance
faded and thin as grass
and there is very little left to prove

ay primo that ditch has been dry since we were kids

in my mind it had always flowed

i want to be young again
like a potrillo in the tall grass
but i am older now
so i turn away
praying por la primavera

tio Willie

tio Willie i think of you
the rattling bus you drove at dawn
the sun
catching it that way
yellow

i think that in that light
all buses are yellow that way
i think of ironies
your skin
becoming yellow
not unlike that bus
as you waited on death
as if it were a child
running late
to your open door
and you were patient

even then
after the skin had turned
you wanted to drive that bus
it may have been
for the quiet times in the garage
alone with the low grunt of the engine

perhaps the bus was best
when there was just
that one child on board
sitting quietly by the window
lost beyond the glass

tio i regret
not being there for your morphine dreams
on those last days
when you saw Anthony
not the dead son you buried

not raw as the ribs of heroin
but alive 'like on t.v.'

sleep finally came tio
we all knew that the poem
would finish itself
returning to its origins

dawn
a rattling bus
yellow
you waiting
patiently
for that child running

zoot suit jesus

zoot suit jesus
drives a monte carlo
a real low pavement sparker
with headlights turned
halogen up to heaven

rims shiny chromed
wink seductively

    "need a ride carnal"

christians that we are
we never decline

with cheap wine and saltines
we take communion
seated on his purple velvet pew

archangel gives her gas
our procession
going 106 down 285

we welcome the rush
it sets our souls in order
as archangel takes us to the altar

but this ain't no wedding
and vows
only get us so far

    "where you taking us carnal"

he turns real coy
his shades resting too cool
on the tip of his nose
the whites of his eyes turn up
as he gives us a hint

"we're going home   way up home carnal   away from hell"
just as the headlights go dim.

bones of my people

i am here
where the faces become a two lane road
one whispers east
to the testimonial light of new day
the other tugs me west
toward the dying red sun of our past

bleached and forgotten
the marrow of my people's bones
has become a map to the mesmerized romantics
who do not listen to the whisper
of their hollow voiceless stare

they ask
when we began running
as a means
to slim our souls

when it was
that we became
so like the red sun that sets
upon our walls

how it was
that we sold
what had just been stolen

and they ask
that we not love the new
more than we hate the old

they whisper
of the oldest bones
that are my people

they say
that these bones are reminders of life
life that was or will never be again

this is what the bones say
they remind us
that we are as flesh to them
as they are marrow to our souls

they beg
that we never forget
who we are

regard for the dead

i have in these past few months
dressed the sun in white
and called it regard for the dead

it was a dream i had
of my abuelita
working in the kitchen
and the way the cortinas
caught the sun
told me she was close to god

the same god i had once
called a carpenter
and asked to build me a ladder
so that i could reach
the white crosses
my dead friend Cristobal
had painted on the cliffs
only so that i could touch them

this is regard for the dead i thought
as i watched my father walk
through dying grass
knowing by the way he looked back at me
that somewhere in that short
distance between us
there were voices trying to learn my name

from the words i awoke
to the sound of piano
where a woman named Maclovia
had been hiding since she was a girl
she only asked that the music continue
asking that something
wonderful be played
with the left hand
so that she could be happy

i could tell you
that i believe god whispers
my own name to me from alfalfa fields
and tells me to repeat it to myself
once for every sun i have seen
and again for every moon i have missed
he tells me to paint the words
that come in between
in regard for the dead

tan poquito el amor luego perderlo

these words come forty years late. the church bells which signaled the end of the second world war have rested their tired hips. they are silent now except for days when the wind comes off the llano and makes them groan. the war ended in a rush of bells, and my mother, in front of her house, a child, began to dance. she has often told me that she never knew why the bells were ringing. she simply knew they were ringing and began to dance.

forty years later she works tortillas in the kitchen. i imagine her, a child, i hear bells scaring the sparrows from the tower where they make their nests. i imagine the sound of bells running through adobe and resting its tired voice in the red willows.

perhaps the bells told the oldest story on earth, men returning from war, children dancing.

my words are those bells my mother heard as a child. they run through me and perch on my memory like a good angle of sun. this letter i write forty years too late is like the bells, destined to fall silent as if i relinquished them in some quiet handshake, as if they were meant to travel by touch.

my mother tells me about the bells that ended the second world war. she is proof that they rang. that for a brief moment she was in love with sound, and years later still in love with their story.

i have made the bells my own. i know that someday they will be lost. that in some dry august they will stop ringing as if they shouldn't have but finally as if they must. i hope that when i am gone someone will ring the bells for whatever adobe still stands, for whatever war has ended, as if something which were lost should be celebrated.

apishapa my heart shaped sister

i.
the apishapa is an old woman
that flows south of pueblo
only when the rains come
wind and thunder for generations
and then finally the rain

my mother waves to me
i am seven
i imagine her seven floors up
waving from her hospital room
i stand in the rainy parking lot
silent except for the far off
southern thunder

my mother has lost
what would have been my younger sister
my mother told me later
that the heart shaped miscarriage
was a girl
younger heart shaped sister
who did not live to be born
into this rain
soft but hardening
as i wave up to the seventh floor

the priest
probably the same priest
who drives all day sunday giving communion
comes to the hospital
in the pockets of his black jacket
holy water
his shoulders wet with rain
he moves quickly to baptize
apishapa my heart shaped sister

ii.
i fish alone
bring what i catch to my mother
she loves fish
the crispy skin   soft flesh
so barely clinging
to the malleable bones

i am alone
except for my mother
a river which always flows
her voice crescendos
over rocks and sand bars
plays off the water
in a loud sad key
her voice is thunder
in the middle of the night

johnny redshirt please call your mother

Lakota radio — 1995

i did not come looking for you
johnny redshirt
but instead a shadow
forming across the badlands
and everything becomes distance
separates on a single thought
as your mother calls you home over the airwaves
her voice assumes
the whole world is listening

the radio becomes the words of poems
the soft words
the hard words
my own mother calling me across the vega
i have fished too long
and she is able to make her voice echo for miles
i ran home johnny
traveling dirt roads
their washboards keeping time with the rhythm
of bearings going out
everything is distance and we are trapped in it

the fences of the badlands
sag and fall
i follow them devotedly
they are
in a word
direction

like you johnny
i want to be missing
not somewhere in the badlands
like a wind trapped in stone
or in your paha sapa littered with signs
no johnny

i have been somebody else's story for too long
i want to be lost like you
and become my own story
which fades in and out on the radio

i want sheep
a garden
walls you can't run electrical wire through
a son who will play football
a son who will sing to his mother
a son who will
like you write his own story
a story
which makes its way into us
the echoes of it
the voice which hopes
the whole world is listening

colcha

i have this dream
always there are footprints
which begin at the window
not the door as they should

i see that door
remember it as green
the clothesline looming
to my right
in the rain
just east of the green door

do you remember
the rain abuelita
it was five years old
with a voice not much louder than mine

voices are important
they call us to church
away from the window
our footprints leading away

    abuelita you may have guessed
    i am having a hard time knowing where to begin
    this problem of finding centers
    consider this a collage
    memories which have not yet
    lined themselves

you smash aspirin
in a spoon
you offer it
and this is love

    the following are the only words i can remember
    saying to my abuelita
        fria me un huevo
        el aaron gramma soy el aaron

thirteen years since your death
i cannot speak to you

we were famous
the way we smoked salems
together in the sala
my small fingers turning brown
then happy with the 89 cents
and what seemed like a long walk
to buy another pack

i believed we were famous
because we only spoke in spanish

      words she invented
          chi hi hitchhike
          grand johnson grand junction
          credit junior credit union
          paul a bentry port of entry

your old house is blue now
they have taken away the green door
demolished the adobe shed
where i played
all that remains is the window
where the dream always begins

      i say they
      i do not know who lives there now

are you proud of me
what i have become
the man who cannot leave
the home where you no longer live

we will return
Michele and i
to be married in spanish
name our first daughter
Amalia

in heaven i am sure you know
how it was that i began to love her
but i must write it for myself
a thank you of sorts

her mother
had wrapped her hair in garas
so the curls would stay
so that when we danced that night
the garas long since untied
i would smell their warmth
as she laid her head upon my shoulder

i never asked
where they got the garas
where their hands
came upon them
began to tear them into thin strips
but i know
they were taken from a quilt

the pink strips
had in my youth
been elephants
blue strips
from the base
where everything rested
white
the original
color of the quilt
you made for me
when i was five

abuelita
up there in heaven
have you seen her hair grow
the way it falls over her back
absorbing the sun

the way it takes in
two of my fingers
as i trace them down her neck

she takes too long curling her hair
this is one of the things i love

> this dream i keep opening and closing
> leads me to ortiz
> the green fields
> and red willows which never leave

i come to the edge of your bed
my cousins are taking pictures
of your last birthday on earth
your position is fetal
my voice is no longer recognizable

> *el aaron gramma*
> *soy el aaron*

> i hold the picture at a distance
> all i can see is the orange
> of the nursing home blanket
> a glaring orange which is thinner than skin

i am young enough
to still love glue
so i build
with glitter and construction paper
tearing strips
glueing them to the
white base of paper
when i finish
i have spelled it correctly
> *happy birthday*

a single pink elephant
rests in the lower corner

i am famous
cousins and aunts congratulate me
there are pictures of me
to prove it
months later
january 11th
i wake during the night
to a ringing phone
my mother
saying o.k.
three times
then we are packing

we do not drive quickly
we do not go to meet the others
at your orange bed

    why does everyone keep saying
    she won't have to suffer anymore

    since that day i have considered this poem
    now as i am writing it i begin to cry

Michele tells me
that we are
who we are by the age of five
that our lives are
from that point on
stitched together
by some pattern we unconsciously follow
she looks at me
as though i am the perfect quilt
i hold her hand
squeeze it tightly
imagine the warm smell of her hair

before you died
they wrapped your feet in a white sabana
filled with dirt

you were born in ortiz
that place in the dream i keep opening
that is where they got the dirt
my uncle spoke of it as being necessary
so that you could die peacefully

the word for me is tierra
the direct translation of which
is dirt
but i prefer to think of it as earth
in some ways
even as my abuelita

atlantic

i.
Michele warns me to look out for black ice
i smile remind her that it is august
but she persists
and encourages me to eat well
she is devoted to the power of vegetables

she leans over at dinner
"eat your peas"
my excuse is that they are green
and perhaps i do not like summer enough
to appreciate that color
i eat only corn

ii.
i go below deck
while my wife on the third deck prays
to her grandmother

the atlantic stretches toward dusk
then turns dark except for the on board lights
occasionally reminding us
that we are miles from land

my wife prays to her dead grandmother
she prays for our marriage
that we will live long
Michele is in love with growing old

iii.
she has beautiful hands
which point out over the atlantic
as though it were a piece of music
she would like to play

her prayer recently finished
we watch the dark atlantic
fall south behind us

iv.
the owl is white
i call it a sea gull

Michele with the beautiful hands
simply calls it white

v.
we are hundreds of miles from land
in the deck lights
the owl becomes an owl
circles moves port side
disappears

we do not know what
to call it
is it her grandmother
letting us know that she heard

i call it the atlantic

vi.
the bird returns
again it is an owl
this time it is prayers heard
darkness and the formerly blue atlantic
cannot keep this from us

will we live long
does the ocean make us more real

we lose the white bird
in the darkness

thirteen ways of looking at a tortilla

i.
among twenty different tortillas
the only thing moving
was the mouth of the niño

ii.
i was of three cultures
like a tortilla
for which there are three bolios

iii.
the tortilla grew on the wooden table
it was a small part of the earth

iv.
a house and a tortilla
are one
a man a woman and a tortilla
are one

v.
i do not know which to prefer
the beauty of the red wall
or the beauty of the green wall
the tortilla fresh
or just after

vi.
tortillas filled the small kitchen
with ancient shadows
the shadow of Maclovia
cooking long ago
the tortilla
rolled from the shadow
the innate roundness

vii.
o thin viejos of chimayo
why do you imagine biscuits
do you not see how the tortilla
lives with the hands
of the women about you

viii.
i know soft corn
and beautiful inescapable sopapillas
but i know too
that the tortilla
has taught me what i know

ix.
when the tortilla is gone
it marks the end
of one of many tortillas

x.
at the sight of tortillas
browning on a black comal
even the pachucos of espanola
would cry out sharply

xi.
he rode over new mexico
in a pearl low rider
once he got a flat
in that he mistook
the shadow of his spare
for a tortilla

xii.
the abuelitas are moving
the tortilla must be baking

xiii.
it was cinco de mayo all year
it was warm
and it was going to get warmer
the tortilla sat
on the frijolito plate

castigando el santo ramon fernandez

i too want to know
that woman who
'sang beyond the genius of the sea'
to see her maiden name
her only dress

i imagine her
as gestures made
a lingering smoke

ramon ramon
this is the woman of whom
we dream
an echo in the eyes of all the men
who mouth her name

dolores maria de los canciones
they sing her name
'and of ourselves and of our origins'
we asked
for one more song

she sang of roads
your road ramon
a guest who walked alone
the earth's lingering pulse
in a town called town

my road ramon
something fainter still
gathering coal
for a fire
which burns my family name

because she sang
we began to pray
and so slowly

turned our saints
upside down
until the prayer answered
the words sung
we turned them back
to that place from which they came

ramon
she is those words
the written names
scrawled upon the trees
the earth's maiden name
some boy's mother
who slowly
sings him home

pronoun poem

it was that
which made them crazy
antelope crazy
running from their shadow everywhere
round and round the mundo pole
that by tuesday
they were chasing it

no not you
not him
her holmes
them holmes
which holmes
all of theirs
went antelope crazy

happy girl walks in
hair sprayed up like a desk lamp
she says to us
no not you
to us holmes
to us she says
can i have my eyes polished

whose eyes
those lovely brown things
i say we can't do yours
somebody something someone
might have everything you need
but we're antelope crazy
     all out of that color

to whom did she run
myself i say to yourselves
the girl is gone
can't blame oneself
herself

she wanted the change
that itself is too bad

now which was the what
that made us crazy
few maybe many know
but nobody   none
no one
on one side of the other
really knows

of course
they would like to say
it was each other one another
blame blame blame
one two three
first second third
such that any could be possible
chances are
neither of the none
but us will know

the title of the poem

will be august
the meadows drying slowly
when i learn that Timmy Sandoval has died
his body thrown 110 feet from his car

the title of the poem will be
where his breath left his body
the descanso
painted metal cross
in the shadow of perlite silos

perhaps Timmy
the title will be the girl you loved
the woman you would have liked
to tell everything to
a soft breath behind the ear
a hand over the lips
or better yet
the title can be the dragonflies
i saw locked together
making love with the wind
your body in love
airborne being pushed past me

your sister in the front pew
i imagine bleeding from her mouth
she says to me

you should taste this
my teeth feel smooth and sweet
and i can't feel my tongue
i love wine aaron
i love to drink

i can taste something
the words of his sister's poem

that first word which she leaves naked
Timmy's shoes in a meadow
filling with rain

untitled (verde)

the locals will come one day
in their pick-up trucks
and begin to dig

they will dig the cedar fence posts
out of the earth
carry off unwanted rock

they will have plans of green
to march the water uphill
in a procession for the dead

as if to say
our dead need
green

they will remove the sage
with its whites and blues
take away the scent after a good rain

they will take away this dirt
which warms so nicely under the sun
so they can lay sod

years from now they will return
with plastic flowers
and comment on how wonderful the green is

marvelous
they will say

i shall answer
the earth is dry
it is
so dry here

trail to los cuates

it is only a matter
of giving the cows a direction
turning them north with our horses
and by that direction
they will know where to go

today we are two days in
moving slowly
with the short winter days
toward los cuates

we eat breakfast
before sunrise
my abuelito frying eggs over a wood stove
dipping a tortilla into his coffee

the co-op thermometer
above his door reads 30 below
and we know from wind
that it is colder than that

the yegua has frost
on the arch of her back
ice forms on her nostrils and down her mane
she refuses the bit
i have warmed in my hands

in the windbreak of a cedar grove
we find a calf
frozen
head motionless between his legs
his mother moves him with her nose
trying to wake him
her udder swelling with milk

we move north
beneath the snow covered mesas

following the herd
through the packed snow
unable to see past the warm vapor
of their breathing
and we must trust that they know the way
that they will move alone without our urging
away from the bugling cow
we could not drive from the calf's side
she will sometime today
realize that the sun
can do her calf no good
and she will move alone
toward los cuates

a letter from my journal to juan

writing from cañada de los tankes
sheep have stopped here again
seems mythical how they know where to stop
do not miss city think of friends
but enjoy being alone

my abuelito used to measure everything in summers
this annual trip to sierra marked his existence
he was first to point out how sheep stop here on their own
have always loved that about this place   good spirits
abuelito does not make trip anymore   too old
wonder if he now learns seasons in reverse
marks his years with return of herd to rancho
assume this is the case
he would not know any other way

made a good pot of beans
had to add water six times
took eight hours to make them on the estufita
will savor them

rained the night before herd got here
had hard time making fire
thought of Pound
'real education must ultimately be limited
to men who insist on knowing. the rest is mere sheep-herding'
never liked that guy
wonder if he knows what got into Ubaldo in 1957
wonder what made him leave his herd in the middle of the night
and run for six miles
before falling off the cliffs of toltec gorge
brujas
ezra might know
do not think he knows what it was like for sheep
lost 86 head
coyotes had a good winter

truly doubt if he knew the smell of Ubaldo's body
when my abuelito found him in river at bottom of gorge
he was only one able to carry him out
do not envy him
cannot imagine feel of skin falling off body

anyway back to pot of beans
had trouble with fire
wished Pound book had been in my possession

lost a borregito somewhere in brazos
must have tired
sheep did not seem to care
but noticed that her ubre was swelling
will begin summer in rincon bonito
where Gabriel killed six deer with six shots
amazing shots
beginning to understand why
if you ask a herder what he is doing
he usually replies making a pot of beans
live from meal to meal
can see that is how it works out here

mosquitoes are like bad dream which am unable to wake from
they tend to stick to the cool wet around the river
makes fishing difficult
but still enjoy the odd angles of my shadow on water
think of grandpa Joe
my last image of him
peaceful and somehow baggy as he stood beneath crab apple tree
odd memory
the baggy part
but knew he had died because of that image
remember him as good fisherman
beautiful unfurling of his line
bamboo rods lonely in garage after his death
think of him often on river
his spirit must be around here somewhere

always walking upstream
because that was the way he did it
can see him sometimes
good fisherman

must sign off for now
please wish everyone my love
take care
adios

the mountains here are named after blood

the mountains will not let
my great grandfather rest

they are the memory unwilling
to resolve itself
or bury its dead

i imagine him
always moving
through the heat
like a blind horse
searching for water

Serafin Serafin
the repetition of his name haunts me
like the clear day
when i found his adobe house
crumbling in the shade of a cottonwood

i saw him being born that day
in one long motion of dust
scattering itself over the llano
never settling

he is those wild horses
the souls of dying men
forever calling family
to stand beside their deathbeds

the mountains are named after blood
the blackness of it growing in cedar
stretching out en la madrugada
like a tired man
calling his son
asking forgiveness
the painful syllables of it
desculpame

the repetition haunts him
his son never comes

Serafin are you that horse
that restless horse which can
never be ridden
driven by blood

this must be the death
you relive
out there in the dust
the memory you try and drink from

a letter to an adopted son

dear Marcos,

We have both made that trip into the valle, the long straight road from Pueblo to Walsenburg, where you think you will travel into the heart of the Spanish Peaks. They rise like two breasts left there to suckle the universe, their milk flowing in two directions. One goes back to our mother, through the desert of Sonora, through the railhead at Celaya, back in time to her womb of water on Tezcoco. She is standing knee deep. Her bare brown feet have gathered mud between the toes. She is from two worlds, like you.

Marcos, you are the milk which flows in two directions, and you are not sure which way to flow. South toward the valle looking for a mother who gave birth to you in a town named after cottonwoods, or south further still to a woman standing knee deep in Tezcoco. So you shuffle through papers of year in which the water kept no record. So that when you stand knee deep in the Conejos you will look at home, the water turning in slow green ripples around your legs, the soft line from your pole searching the bottom of the river for a piece of your history.

i watch as you read the scales of a fish as though they were maps to somewhere else. The red streak on the fish's belly tells you that she is spawning, that within her belly there are orange eggs which she will lay beneath a rock, and that they will hatch without knowing their mother. You hold her, this mother, in your hand; you feel the turning of her spine as she slips from your hand into the green water. i know now, why you let her go.

santa fe girl

the scent of rain drips
like your sandal

dangling
from your brown foot

framing
my attention

as it creeps up the
curves of your leg

like low clouds
rolling over the plaza

your hair clinging
in slow trickles

as you rise and run
from the rain

leaving me
dry and alone

and oh how i need
a sip

the distance between us

is the silent fingering of a flute
the music
which will not reach our ears in this lifetime
the words
which separate ten years from my brother and i
the memories i have as a child
of a young boy walking toward the sandstone cliffs
to paint his blue hearts
they are my only memory
all i can say

they are what i point out to you
the blue hearts whose paint was not symbolic
simply the only paint you could find

you tell me how phoenix lies ahead
how you hope the sun
can heal you in twenty days

you are my oldest brother
who wishes he could paint
the entire mountain the same shade of blue
because you loved a woman
a place
too much

you sit in silence
the distance between us
the words i cannot say
which erode against our minds
in the slow turning of a single day

instructions on how to write a pinche suicide note

let me tell you how to write a pinche suicide note
it aint no ten cent poem written in red ink pendejo
a la madre it's more than that ese
it's making love to a bottle
sucking the last drop like some desperate dog
it's cruising up and down the same street
for days
looking
you know   eyes all around
nothing seen but cracked sidewalks
and some fourteen year old mamas boy
who thinks he knows how to get stoned
orale
that is step one

step two
shape it with your hands
caress that son of a bastard
drive your nails in until it turns into
that cheap ass courage it takes
to pull that pinche trigger
or tie that pissy knot around your neck
as you look into your own eyes
blank as smoke
smiling   asking
who's pinche winning now
orale   that is step two

step three
get your selfish ass out of bed
take a drag toke or swig
whatever makes the words come
mill 'em around like some little tangle haired girl
drawing circles on the pavement

hop scotch or die
playing jacks with your pinche life
pick 'em up quick carnal
before they melt in the sun
orale
that is step three

step four
pray the rosary
they say praying to the virgin
is more bullseye than praying to el hijo
tell her how you tried
how you shot the shit into your veins
until you couldn't get off the ride
that has finally come
and then   only then
you're ready to sign
with red ink
what else

untitled

you those poets i see
among a perimeter of eyes
forgive that i am not the books i read
or that i find pain in my mother's wish
that she not die during the winter
or that i write her a poem
as an epitaph

i cannot write of the living
as though they were dead

i am
in the vernacular of my life
ascared to die
to write a poem where i find
mortality in those things
that flow with blood
and learn to walk
as though they were afraid
of having to learn the motions
again in their old age

i am tired of this road
where my only shade
is the shadow of a hawk
which circles and never
flaps her wings
knowing that i will stumble

can you forgive me
for the poems i will not let you see
those poems i wrapped in green plastic
and left in the branch of a cottonwood
these will better say
why the water in the glass is so still
why i will not let you drink

why it would be better that we died here
us poets who look too far
into mirages for our sustenance

it would be better
that we died of love
or an emotion
we cannot yet name

discussions with a ghost of his own creation on why he cannot go north

these roads at dusk
in the gathering darkness
are golden
yet Juan my left eyed friend
remembers their darkness
things eyes could not see
a dark figure his son
moving north
against the oncoming headlights

Juan's silence
the constant refilling of his pen
how he tends to suck on his turquoise ring
his poems about open yards
fathers calling
out to their sons
what men build
between the callings and
the departures

Juan moves
with his runners form
along the washed out arroyos
over the bare wind swept hills
looking for the white doored attic
he calls north
looking for something in the carved 'i love you's'
of the sandstone cliffs

in these many months
that i have not seen him
he has had a communion
with the wind

which told him to stay
to not go north
told him to stay with his first snow
which refuses to melt

cinco de mayo

i look through a book of names
as thick as a man's fist
looking for the name of a man
who died as though he were sleeping
Jose Angel Ortiz

my finger finds his name
on the ninth panel
of the vietnam veteran's memorial
a cloud of dust
and the faintest flickering of light
when the grenade put his name
into the black granite

i was not there
i was not born yet
i know he died
hardly looking dead at all
when my father in law
identified Jose Angel Ortiz
he looked like he was asleep

still this is not
1968 and the faintest flickering of light
it is 1998
and people believe
cinco de mayo
is about cruising
federal bouelevard

cinco de mayo
is not about cruising
not about what flag we wave
but about memory
i offer
that it is about names

Jose Angel Ortiz
was returned to texas
wrapped in stars
not a marine
not even alive
his mother not concerned
with which flag covered
her boy

cinco de mayo
a boy cruises federal
until his car runs out of gas
he pushes it slowly toward the station
he does not make it
a bullet to the head
a boy dies outside a convenience store

i have already forgotten his name
cinco de mayo
it was the fifth of may
can you remember that boy's name
did his mother wrap him in a flag
did he die as though he were asleep

i rub the name
Jose Angel Ortiz
onto a white piece of paper
the pencil catching fragments
of letters and partial names
which surround the name
i have come looking for
it is a beautiful name
say it with me
Jose Angel Ortiz

coal train

Hay algo mas triste en el mundo
que un tren inmovil en la lluvia? Pablo Neruda

i am writing in Neruda green
as the world's saddest train
stretches south
toward walsenburg's winter hills

years ago we sat here for hours
as ambulance and police
pulled the body of a deaf boy
from the tracks

seasons ago
the gondola cars of coal
had shadows
that rocked in the sunlight
where iron could dance
and the days would lead

what faint call
did that deaf boy hear
on which beat did he join in
on which step did his partner
coal train
hear him scream

my father
every time we passed these tracks
he remembered the boy
who stopped traffic so many years ago
during a time
when we were all boys
counting box cars 1 2 3 with their
clip clip churn
as they rolled slowly by
and as men

like Neruda
we regard this train standing in the snow
as the saddest thing on earth

we count gondola cars filled with coal
and remember stories
recreate pieces of coal
thrown from moving trains
we are boys
waiting beside the tracks
collecting coal
in burlap potato sacks
telling everyone the black stones
are gifts collected in the cold

at what point in my life
i wonder now
when did my father stop remembering
the deaf boy
at what point in my life
had i learned the lesson
everything that moves
does not necessarily dance
during which snow
did the train stop on the hillside
the cars like pale footprints
climbing   climbing with sacks of coal
until the last of them
is gone from sight
finally underway
clicking slowly south

december 20th

The wounds were burning like suns at five in the afternoon . . .
Ah, that fatal five in the afternoon! Federico Garcia Lorca

december 20th
the setting sun has turned the sky to a color
i cannot describe
december 20th
a boy somewhere inside me
searches the llano for a borregero
the day is december 20th
the llano with its snow
is cold and white

on the 20th of december
a borregero
brings his flock home
on this day
women will come to screen doors
and wave at the passing borregero
it is december 20th
when i join in behind the herd
to hear a story of a horse so fast

Roger Arellano
rode a palomina horse
on december 20th 1979
i wonder if that same horse
carries a borregero from this life
today the sky
is a bloodshot eye
a face that has had too much wine

yesterday
i believed that clouds
painted on stained glass windows

it is the 20th of december
our borregero tells me of a horse so fast

it outran the rain
not every december is happy
not every memory of a borregero
is a good one

a borregero lives alone
and once a year
usually in december
Roger Arellano
on a day that wasn't the 20th of december
made me believe that
stained glass clouds were sheep

a borregero lives alone
and once a year drinks too much wine
this is one of those unhappy decembers

every day of the year
including december 20th
a borregero smokes lucky strikes

a borregero dies in june
he is carried from this life on a fast horse
i learn of his death on december 20th
at this moment
i don't know if i'm a man or a boy

as a boy
during one of those good decembers
Roger lit a fire beneath a solitary cedar tree
still a borregero knows
that in the mind of children
it can always be a good december
today the sky
is an apple skin peeled with an old timer knife

on december 1st
these lonesome borregeros tell women they love
that they will be home on the 20th

in my boy's mind
i remember Roger Arellano
at my abuelita's funeral
he asked my father for five dollars
he used it on wine
this was a bad december

on which winter night
did Roger Arellano shovel through a blizzard
only to find that come morning 23 sheep

ultimately in the december of your life
you will compare yourself
to an old wagon

i believe the day was
the 20th of december
Roger shoveled all night
but come morning
23 sheep died
in the deep snow drifts

december 1997
i imagine Roger's name
in the local paper
perhaps today
the sky is the color of heaven
reflecting off a glass of wine

does someone mark the date
when a man remembers
on the 20th of december

i think of that horse almost every day
Roger told me that the rain fell
and the horse ran
the horse ran so fast
that on this day almost 20 years later
i still remember that only its tail got wet

not all memories
are as good as that one
maybe the sky is the color of an alcoholics skin

by all the calendars
it was december 20th
with the sun going down
Roger Arellano was his name
he told me once
i can't remember the day
that he saw two women
skinny dipping
Roger told me
that they call
new mexico
the land of enchantment
because of those two women

not all memories are bad
not every december
is snowy

december 20th
i am reminded
that i am fading
toward that undefinable sky
this is why men
carve their names in trees
delaying their own decembers

Roger Arellano showed me a name
carved into a tree in 1933
no month was given
we used an old timer knife
the month was june
we carved our own names in that tree
each letter stretching
a scar marking this and two other's lives

usually i do not feel so mortal
but today is december 20th
my friend died the previous june
the sky to my left
on this 20th day of december
as i travel north
is the color of yesterday
today the herd is still on the llano
i search white hills
for our borregero his herd
i see neither

a borregero during a previous june
guides his herd home
he passes a tree with names carved in it
on that june day
i imagine Roger
rode the palomina horse
he had outlived

a borregeros name
grows on that tree
today is december 20th
a boy with curly hair
searches the llano for a borregero
on december 20th
that same boy looks again
as a man he sees nothing
a boy searched for a borregero
a man on the road home
searched for a borregero
on december 20th
he thought the sky looked like fire

i like the way the singer of the song tells jesus

that he has left his boat in the sand
para buscar otro mar
this singer must be Leandro
who knew the firing order
of every engine ever built
who one day in august i helped
move rows of copper wheat
armful after armful away
from the falling sprinkler water
he laughed
and i remember that too
all teeth and beard

Leandro
vecino whose wheat
always grew taller than ours
you had a way about your smile
like a hand plunged into the soil
like seed rolled from palm to palm
like pouring water

i did not help plant
that spring when you died
when they found you
without breath
legs half in the dirt
torso twisted tourniquet tight
your jacket caught in the machinery
the tractor idling
with a low watchful groan
each cylinder
firing in perfect time

every spring in the valle
is windy
i use the color brown

to describe where i am from
by june we will use
the color green
to tell the daily rains which
river of color to fill
which field is like copper
which is like gold

in august after the rains
with the wheat in circular swaths
as autumn grows nearer
i think of Leandro
how i helped him one day
carry armfuls of cut wheat
how that was the last time i saw him
all teeth and beard
laughing like the wind
which comes every spring

poem in c minor
for memory

what i remember is imperfect
a yellow house
a large man with possessed hands
my sister with her reedy saxophone
my brother with his dented coronet
yet amid all the half memories
the sinful yellow house still stands

i come early
while the dew is still clinging
to the earth in the half dark
of what i call a malignant blue morning

amid my breath
i grease the tractor
the rows of cut alfalfa
turn in 1/2 mile circles around me
the sinful yellow house
sits quiet

his name was Polk
six foot of polyester
big hands
jive collars
god shed his grace on thee
rhythm which would
bring the auditorium
into the spell of his moving hands

in that yellow house
he laid those same hands
ran those same hands
over the smooth skin
of his daughter
a shadow

which simply put
would become the rumor
of the yellow house

the house itself
comes to me in fragments
of isolation caught between
the shadows of the san juans
and the sangre de cristos
each pulling
not for day or night
but each
for its own redemption
a young girl's voice
a tormented song
devoid of grace

it was Polk
with his suicide in that yellow house
which made me believe
that the mountains
named for saints
and christ's blood
have their own sort of vengeance

the mountains are everyone's
last image of this place
they remind us
that we forget so easily
what does not haunt us

her daddy led the band
with its dented coronets
and reedy saxophones
which somehow
beneath these mountains
became a disconnected melody
about a man who sinned inside
a yellow house

in the early mornings
as i work the fields
around that yellow house
i can feel the sangre de cristos
the darkness of their cedar
as they give up the sun
to the san juans fading darkness

a young girl from back then
a woman now
must see these mountains
as a soulless
far off place

i look through old pictures
Polk stands right foot forward
his band dressed in blue
in a semi-circle around him
i focus on his eyes
blank as an empty yellow house
his blue band silent
and smiling around him

a river poem for someone i never knew

my mother
asked if i could
write a poem
about someone i never knew
Aurelio
abuelito whose grave
we always clean second
but find nonetheless
marking 1957 the year
your heart gave out
on the way home from the movies

stories of you surface
like fish feeding
as you stand knee deep in the river
a great fisherman
never coming home empty handed
yet perhaps too generous
giving away most of your catch
on the way home

abuelito
i know you
here on the conejos
in the early mornings
among the bird filled
river banks
the silent dew
and the slightly louder
river
which when the fish
are biting
becomes an artery
never giving out

there are rippled pools
beneath the trees and branches

each growing circle
of a fish's passing
like a fading pulse
of that night
when your heart
failing
planted its generous but weak
kiss on your sons
each with a heart which is
partly yours
men willing to give away
every fish in the river

generous abuelito
your hand guides me
to the break
in the river
where the white
of a faster moving current
throws its arms
around a rock
flows away
calmly   smoothly
beneath a willow
whose shadow hints at
a fish who almost rises
but does not
creates no pulse
in my river
the way i know you
forty years after
in a poem
a very old memory
not quite knowing
but audible
like a heartbeat
a river moving

for the intentions we hold within the silence of our hearts

i pray for my tio Willie
that Mary
will let him rest his tired neck
take him from those fields
of my dreams
where he rakes hay
for all the days that heaven
can offer
i pray for him
because my abuelo
didn't want him
to sell his llanos
to any gringo
but he did
y pa que
to drive a bus
sometimes i pray for that bus
for its safe passage
that when it gets cold
some kid
will yell out to his uncle
turn up the heat uncle Willie
and always it will become warm
for this i pray

i often ask that one
of my fathers two dreams
will come true
that someday
beef prices will rise
i pray
that on his weekly trips
on the eastbound road
to la junta

the sun will not blind him
as it rises above
the hills which seem to sway
brown in every season
he has two jobs
his neck hurts
he refuses to take aspirin
in some ways
i am like him
and for this
i also pray

for my mother
who forty-five years ago
lived in memphis
i pray that she
will not be sad
like the day
the a.m. radio
said elvis had died
she cried almost silently
but very visibly
mt. blanca was to our left
near the summit
there was still snow
we were travelling due east
but in the front seat
of our caprice classic
there was just the radio
memphis on my mother's mind
and a few prayers
for everyone who was sad

i always have silent intentions
for Roger Arellano
he told good stories
always there was a fast horse
always there was some form of love
always there was the smoke of lucky strikes
he wore thick leather chaps
his legs were so thin
he rode well
drank too much
herded sheep with his two dogs
poncho and smokey
for him i pray because
when i was young
once a week
he was my imagination

i pray
for Michele my wife
her sense of memory
she associates
hot tea with her grandma
recalls playing in snow
when she was five
plays it on her flute
i pray we will have a house
where we can see every star in the sky
i pray silently
for a long life
for a good week
lord hear my prayers
silent as they are

3515 wyandot

i return to this house
like a flower to its seed
a young girl
the earth giving and dark
as i plant yellow roses
with my grandpa Epi

in the morning
before the smell
of tortillas and potatoes frying
my grandpa will dress
in his blue uniform
his hat so perfectly stiff
my abuelita and i
lying side by side
watching him go
his hand like a flower in bloom
as he waves goodbye

the roses
the roses you and your grandpa planted
my grandmother says to me
have grown so beautiful
against this south facing brick wall
i smile because i have grown too
returning in all seasons
to see the roses
sometimes living
sometimes so patiently
clinging waiting for
a warm southern sun

grandpa Epi
with his blue uniform
my brother and i
playing in the long back yard

my grandma
calling to us from the kitchen
the smell of green chile
so delicately resting
on her skin

i have grown
my grandpa Epi
has died
yet i return to
3515 wyandot
the smell of candles and perfume
knowing my abuelita
has worked all day
on her hands and knees
cleaning floors
her santos   mary   and   jesus
watching her penance
the roses have gone wild
i return again
a flower year after year
blooming its way back
to a seed sown
childhoods ago
the house in other's hands
that do not light candles
or clean for santos
the roses
so yellow and old
have bloomed
and broken from the lattice

no singing voices
from the rooms
smoke and
the sound of a hungry cat
breathe from the carpet
in a house
i no longer recognize

no sound from the kitchen
the gas range has
no words or scents to offer
this house with its cracking walls
some would say
has given up
its good spirits
the songs and stories
are a vacant back yard
with cans and broken tables
a sad trail of seed

i   who as a girl
planted yellow roses here
begin to cry
i seek the roses out
against the south wall

the roses have gone wild
no longer a part of the house
they reach like the hands
of one hundred spirits
in full bloom
waving goodbye   for Michele

mixed metaphor (inspirational hymn)

now this poem has got to be read
with a voice down low
like a guitar string way outta tune
then she'll sound good
real good
and the pen will burn through the pulp

it's like driving way too fast
you build it up until you're going
a hundred and forty three
and your head can't be pulled
from the seat cover
your eyes peeled to the horizon
your hands dripping poetic juices
on the page interspersed with blood
and it tastes good
real good

the girl to your right
she screams for more
more of those words that leave her tangled
until she explodes in your palm
and the car goes wrong
you struggle with the wheel
her mechanized hips
they sway and they tail
and it just aint right

so you drive until the road turns black
and you begin to think
think   think harder
as the rubber burns in your soul
gripping for idle asphalt
it goes on and on
like a tick and a tick and a tick and a tock
until you get it right

and it feels good again
real good
like that original chord
and the girl comes back
strong as a trooper
and she wants to see your poetic license

salems

i am alone among the Spanish voices
and the smell of salems

winter after itself

a first frost
white except
the roads out
brown and damp
summers faint feet
still upon them

local paper
lists most
influential people
of the valley's
century

names thump
against my eyes
unfamiliar
like someone
getting off a train
71 years ago
staying

Warshauer
50,000 sheep
rich antonito
past tense
words like *was*
antiseptic qualifier
for the paper's
image of
my home

i am afflicted
by my tendency
to revise
to know
that Warshauer

got his lambs
from lanolin handed
herders
brown hands
that must have
waved their
herds goodbye
onto the
northbound train
out of antonito

be back
next week
he said
when they sell
i'll have your money

poverty looks
through wrought iron
at Warshauer's mansion
the paper notes
this home
and a lesser one
which were
built by
a rich man
with vaudeville nieces
also mentioned

i revise
what my eyes
tell me
northbound trains
that never returned
watch the horse's
mane weep snow
i revise
like Pablo

for the broken handed
for a newspaper
so history filled
with truth
that only
a snow
like today's
only winter
could revise
that lie

the gifts the mountain kept

today the blue mountain
is breathing something hot
into the still dawn
a reddish orange
woven through a visiting
storm of gray clouds

twenty two years ago
an august
i am six years old
that is when i heard
about the mountain
and a plane
that lost altitude
one december
its belly full of toys
a crash

this is the promise
my father spoke of
*jito   if we climb it
you can have all the toys
up there*

he is not the same
father of 1977
but the mountain
no   that too is different

there is a story
of two navajo
who disappeared into
the summer mountain
named after its
winter self
blanca

they are not lost
but look for a gift
winged and
capable of flight
a silver four prop
with tons of toys
two pilots
never found

there is a telling
of how they changed
how their faces spoke
of something spiritual
how the wind
left a historical record
like rings of a tree
written into their skin

so too my father
and i have changed
less so in our skin
but in what
we no longer mention
he does not speak of climbing
like the younger father of 1977
there is nothing said
of the battery operated toys
strewn at 13,800 ft.

the pattern here
is twos
a boy and his father
two pilots
and two navajo
sent to find us all

i would like to ask them
what they found there

if their search party
would bring closure
to a december
when things
stopped flying
or to an august in 1977
the day elvis died
and the scattered toys
became gifts

the answer
is what the mountain
gives back
what it cannot hold
the snow it shakes
from its flanks
the gifts it keeps
like promises

independence day

for a moment the dead dog
i have named independence day
is a motionless train
in a nameless montana town
a river held at her source
waiting wanting
to continue her run home

the dead dog
tied to the fence
with a bullet in his head
is married to a thousand different metaphors
wanting waiting
to come back to life

at first it does not feel right
that i think of my family
when i look at this dog
independence day
and later think of my friends

the dog is all of them leaving
released by the gradual turning
of the train's wheels
a river tumbling the first rock of spring
in its current

there is a woman
with a thousand fingerprints on her shoulder
who stands in the darkest corners near the juke box
replaying a-13 a-13 a-13
estoy sentado aqui
no one will ask her to dance
a man at the bar mumbles
that she used to be good with words
"effortlessly como nada   on command"
"pues que paso"

i stop listening
make up my own story
name her independence day
and it is 1977
the longest day of the year
she is no longer young
god has sold her a face
which wants and waits
for a man
who still refuses to dance with her

for Torrez
the dead dog is arizona
her heat held by a rope
unable to make its way back
into colorado

from the top of the mesa
he calls the san juans
the east coast of his country
the farthest he or
arizona's heat
will ever venture

he seems disappointed
that the mountains are named after a saint
like he wants more
it is easy enough to imagine
what more might be
sunlight
warmer hands
familiar dust
blood which flows in two directions

he waits
points west
says it again
over there that's my home

Juan you hammer in the rain
sink set
my left eyed friend
who does not know which is worse
the oregon rain
or the rain suit

you waste no motion
sink set
words like the rhythmic pings
of steel on steel
as you build light
on long straight highways
where the indian grass
is always golden
sink set
remembering

the tips of your thumbs
have callused
this is your most beautiful poem
the way you have worked yourself
toward the light
moving slowly
the word in spanish
despasito
sink set

    for a moment
    we have become that dead dog
    finally set in motion
    as he herds the sheep from the tall grass
    of Lobato's field
    where our minds
    have brought him back to life

Marcos
your mother's shadow

is walking through cottonwoods
miles from her body
and she is not the beautiful woman
who talks to you in your dreams   but real
drinking coffee
with both hands
wanting to talk to you too
words like
how have you been
you have my eyes

you have her eyes
i am convinced

we are all
haunted by our mothers
the way they are impossible to write about

my own mother
is untouchable this way
so i wait for visions of her
tucking in children that are not her own
making her way through rooms
lit by 60 watt bulbs
so i can draw her face
from every imaginable light
and find that shadows do not exist
the way they should
in words

my last run at independence
1989 i thought that seattle's rain
could wash things away
little things
like wanting to leave
antonito's cracked sidewalks
but as i sat in that motionless train
a thousand miles between seattle

and the town i was running from
i wanted the train to move south
making its way back across the divide
to flow in a different direction

there was something
in the northern water's color
which did not move but wanted to

i missed this dry earth
these last days when spring cannot decide
and the dust is older than you or i can remember

you being the dog
independence day who i stand over
in the way people stand
when they are afraid to move

someone has tied independence day to a fence
where he sits motionless
waiting and
wanting to move